Lycanthrope

SASHA MADSEN

Fulton Books, Inc.
Meadville, PA

Published by Fulton Books 2021

ISBN 978-1-63860-364-1 (paperback)
ISBN 978-1-63860-365-8 (digital)

Printed in the United States of America

To Sean Francis Ryan:
The strength in my bones and the charm in my smile.

Golden Baby

Golden baby and gentle soul,
Thank you for reaching down as I float through this inky hell.
I won't reach the surface without you.
No one ever taught me to swim.

I relaxed in my trusting way as I saw the striking white of your palms,
But I never thought to wonder
Were you reaching for my hands to pull me up
Or reaching for my skull to keep me down until it all went dark?

Light There

My face is blurred and fuzzy like a swear on the radio,
Obscured by a dusty veil I pin to my hair.
I complain no one can make me out,
Yet each day, I pin the veil back in its place.
I press my fingers to my face and even I can't stand how cold they are.
I think I was married once but to what I forget.
Nothing good if it is gone.

Outlander

It's not a lie when I strap the garish plague mask to my head.
Without a doubt, I have been sick for a while now.
And after all,
It is nice to finally have some color.
You glare at my pale, gnarled fingers,
But you know damn well I creeped you out beforehand anyways.
I stand with the other birds on the misty peak now,
Only I am facing the wrong way.

For All the Times I Never Could

My lupine baby,
Hide under the curtain of my hair and inside my arms.
My cold fingers will stroke your trembling cheek,
And we will make those fangs retreat to your gums again.
They will not hurt you anymore, gentle baby.
I will not send you away with this fight unfinished.
When you feel well enough to be separated from my arms,
Make your way to my fire and warm yourself.
I will grab my pitchfork.
Those who have long strove to hurt you will wake to a red-colored
    sun.

Gallinaceous

Anguish is a wind that whips through my creaky old house.
The notches of my enervated spine transfix me,
Keeping me in my limp state.

Raw and bloodless, I blend all into one color.
My throbbing knuckles scrape the hard floor as I fold.

Why didn't my creator give me eyes that can see through
The offensive pollution bleeding into the sky.

I want to shine a light through the wicked smog
To see if a halo appears on the crown of my head.

Such a celestial circle where no grief can live.
My maker will finally elevate me to a land of folly adventures.

Where for Art Thou

My love, my grace, my soul,
Who promised to love me until I was old.
I never meant to lay before you this way.

Exquisite or bland: which did you first think I was?
Were the same stars in your eyes the moment I died?

You have shown me the physical secrets of the world,
And the sacred, arcane soul of a man.
Kiss me in your saintly way.
I will leave your side purified.

Nightcrawler

Long-limbed creature articulately weaving.
Prized predator, always scheming.
In his dim abode he awaits your trusting steps,
Counting to himself the minutes you have left.
He owns open eyes much too excitable for a commonplace appetite
And needle legs creeping ever too precisely for mortal ears.

I could not blame you, you know
For not bracing for his lunge.

His venomous bite is like whorls of filthy ink penetrating fresh milk.
He savors your paralysis and the whimper that escapes your lips.
I am watching him watching you,
And I just cannot tear my eyes away.

Axilla

They tell me to write what I know.
Why should you care what I have seen?

Fellow traveler, I will tell you, I feel scores above my own age.
I know what it is to silently plead for approval
And beg the eyes that find you to see what all the others missed.

I have judged the world with youthful wisdom as they have judged me,
And I can't find the answers I am looking for in my own heart.

How can I reach you from a page I have never touched?

This path is yours alone to walk.
There will always come a time when you will reach a fork and some-
        one will have to leave yours to follow their own.
No one has ever said that on this walk you cannot stop for a moment
        to plant some flowers
Or draw pictures in the dirt with a stick.
Gather yourself:
Find your strength in your pain,
And do not struggle so hard to conceal your demons from others
For if they expect to be able to love you, they will have to love them, too.

Never injure the hearts of others.
You never know when the poison of your pain will come back to you.

Do not let anxiety be your mortal enemy.
When your knees buckle and your hands begin to shake,
Consider that your spirit wants to tango with your body
And that you are your own only worthy partner.

Sweetness,
I am here when you need me.
All my words are another part of a long letter I am writing to you.

Thinker

Raissa traveled the world, looking for hearts that looked like her own. These hearts were her only possessions. She would carry them in a sack over her shoulder, held up by an elderly curved stick. Her soft white dress flowed as she walked along the finest stone paths of the planet. Through the unforgiving storms of the relentless sun, she walked on, knowing that there were more hearts out there for her.

Raissa met single mothers keeping the fireplace warm for their babies and working-class men with lovely, calloused hands. She met soldiers who smiled with ghosts on their backs and artists who spoke in languages only they could understand. Musicians whose fingers who were raw from plucking strings and contortionists who could fold up into a frayed suitcase. All these wonderful, glamorous people were all born under the same sky and therefore, could be reached.

These people and Raissa got together as often as they could, always with food and laughter. With compassion and generosity, she would win their hearts and take them along with her on her next journey.

She liked the weight of the pack she carried. She felt safe knowing they were always near.

The hills puffed their bellies to the sky just for Raissa, waving their poppies at her like an elegant woman's slim, manicured hand. Raissa bit her lower lip and inhaled deeply, nose tickling at spring's cheap perfume of blooms and day-old rainstorms.

Chuckling to herself, Raissa got onto her knees and untied the secure knot of her pack. She grabbed handfuls of hearts, pressing them against her chest. Some spilled out of the side, tumbling into her lap. All of them staining her white dress red.

Polish

It seems like all of my life I have been trying much too hard for boys
    to like me.
Curling my hair wasn't so bad,
But before long, I was choking on glitter.
Men would not fall for glitter.

Schadenfreude

This kind of pleasure should not come at someone else's misfortune.
For a nice girl anyways.
But maybe I am not the pristine sort we all thought I was.
It seems to me like a phantom hand from the great beyond pushed
     you down
And you fell hard like a toddler.
While all those more mature than us attempted to help you back up,
I laughed out loud.
Amen.

Siberia

Everyone describes hell as this burning place,
And we imagine a pit full of fire.
Frost can burn as well.

Myself,
I have always imagined hell as a frozen wasteland
Where you cannot even call for help as your teeth have cracked for
　　constant chattering.
Friendless and without a touch of vegetation.
What sort of thing could survive out there?
Your shoulders tense and your eyes wince as the constant wind
　　screams,
Scolding you for your past misdeeds.

Avenue

Atomic bombs and nuclear holocausts,
Not to mention starvation, global warming,
And our nations latest economic swan dive.

Our parents wonder why we listen to sad songs as we plainly beg for
an escape.
Alas,
Even pop culture's best is littered with death.

But hey,
Billboards are screaming at me that everything will be find as long as
I do not have a plain face.
I suppose I should trust that.
I just hope I can afford a safe house.

Didn't See

I went into the market, intending to get a pound of chocolate
And instead left with a basket of peaches.
Maybe I wasn't paying attention,
Lost in the clouds once again.
Or maybe I didn't know what I needed.
It isn't always a snack I would prefer.

You Learn

Light is breaking through the ripples of the crystalline surface
And I am releasing as the green sea surrounds me—
Holding me as I never thought I would be.
I have brought this dawn as I have deceived my own self.
The sea never whispered promises to me.
Sometimes we smile as we drown,
Forgetting we were not meant to breathe under the sea.

Poor Me

Each of us in the whole world are bred from and for something
     entirely different from each other.
Some of us may never feel the sting of wholehearted desperation,
But we must try with each action
To take the lemons that life gives us
And accept that they do not taste as forgiving as grapes.

Fine Art

Accepting yourself exactly as you are is a civil war at best,
But you cannot bring in an ally without acceptance.
The lines seem a tragic catastrophe.
A leaning skeleton for your body of work,
Holding up flaky color.
Maybe no one lingered at the gallery.
That does not mean you cannot make fine art
With only blue crayons.

Of a Storm

I miss my home
Where the sky is made of flames
And every road dips and winds with the same chaos of an angry
snake.
The winters sting,
And the summers, too.
My father's house is too loud,
But I can't rest in the quiet.
Our private metropolis never halts our unionized production of
shouting and stomping like a thunderstorm.

Not everyone could survive in a storm,
But I have been struck enough to appreciate the sunshine.

Brute

All the lights in my house are off and sometimes it is more than I can take. It would be pointless to describe to you the features of my face as I would not know them if I saw them. Why should you?

"I will be brutal." They should have said that before their stinging kiss. Now I cannot sleep, and I shiver when it isn't cold. My loved ones tell me to look for sunshine, but I wish they would draw me a map. I am lost enough as it is.

I am trying to rise in the dense, breathless quiet of the morning, but all of my bones are cracking and it makes me think I was not made to rise from my bed. I do not know who I inherited my brain from, but they have some explaining to do. I have been held hostage for long enough, and eventually, I am going to get up from my bed.

"Rise, my sweet creature…" I wish an angel would call to me, but I know I am not flesh and bone for nothing. I can reason with myself once I return my mind to its factory setting. My biggest fault is that I have spent too much time waiting for someone else. An angel in a land of flesh. Why would an angel wander here?

I am as brutish as a wolf in winter and yet I need my present circumstances explained to me. Maybe if I was more forgiving, I would have formed a pack. Perhaps I never really wanted one, and that is why I still live alone. Maybe, Reader, in some lone way, being a brute is okay.

Depth

Beauty is like a scar:
A perfect accident that will single you out for life.
Some people are attracted to it
While others cannot stand to look.
You might be disfigured after all,
Judging by the colors you are wearing underneath it.
The difference between beauty and a scar
Is that it is unacceptable to judge someone by a scar
Even though you wear both forever
And they may never change
So you will not always be able to smile about it.

Nationale

I do not know if I have ever known what I've wanted.
How could I know when I was born without answers?
All I can say
Is that I want to make like Daphne
And tunnel my roots deep into the earth as I bask in the delicious
   sunlight.

Rewild

Underneath all the layers of my face
Are a million worries and questions.
But you accept confidence at the stain of my lips.
Sometimes I'm glad, and sometimes I wish I would come across
    someone who could see right through me.

Someday I will find my way back.
I will return to my natural state.
I just have to discover what it is.

Nugacity

As human beings, we are all flakes of snow.
Some will be photographed
To be kept in a frame as art.
Some will be the first to fall.
Some will be held high in a child's wonderful palm.
Some will be held closer to the ground, stained with mud.
But we are all individually exquisite
With a purpose to fulfill
Before we melt.

Endymion

There has always been a red string tied to your finger and mine,
Forever taut between us.
When you travel further from me, I feel its tenacious grip cutting off
 my circulation and leaving me violet.
When you wander closer, I wind it up, hoping to guide you even nearer.

Your hand comes to me first
And before I see anything else, I am imagining planting kisses on
 those slender, lasting fingers.

The quick glimpse of your chest and collarbone is striking,
But diminishes far too fast.
My spirit is weightless,
Wandering hopelessly in the air.

Your chiseled face was carved from marble
By the generous hand of someone imagining a god.

You have returned to forge an Igor in me out of heat and anguish.
The flames are burning too high
And I will combust to nothing.

I have met your eyes now, and they are too much.
The entire night sky swells into one reachable place
And so I am overcome and could cry.
Cup my cheek and keep me steady.

You are the glory of the universe.
This red reel is my life's work.
I will be the natural guard of your sanctuary,
And you may command my heart any way you please.

Thunderstone

Some are in awe of it, though I am scared.
Still, I have this noble young heart that betrays me regularly.
It hurls me out to be sucked under the tires of others when I would
    rather be in bed reading.
When will I stop owing my goodness to others and pay it to myself?
My debt to myself is higher, though I will put it off until the sharks
    come.

I want to be struck down upon by a great storm.
I want to carry the spiderwebbed tendrils of lightning onto my skin
And allow my human heart to spill out,
Replaced with elephantine fury.

Diapason

I can hear you from here.
The wind has carried your melodious voice to me
And your letter has passed through my shaking fingers.

I love you, too.

There are many forms of love
And a brave young heart has felt all of them.

Maybe one day it will cause me pain,
But I just cannot turn any of them away today.

Applesauce

Nothing but nonsense lives inside of this tiny head.
Knotted lines and unfinished paintings.
Screams I have not yet screamed
And a circus of people I am not sure of.

How do you live with a universe made of applesauce in your head?
You can eat your way out.

Gnathonic

Do not force yourself to love me if it does not come naturally.
Believe me, I understand.
There's been nights I have fallen asleep not loving myself at all.
And yet mornings I have woken up happy to be me.

With battles like that waged so brutally across every continent
Why do we try so hard to win over everyone else?
You yourself are enough,
And I am enough, too.

Mother of Snow

You have kissed every creature,
Loved far and wide.
I said I preferred summer.
You never left my side.

Mother is howling,
Calling us to play.
She wants to see us now.
She cannot visit every day.

Chione is my mother.
I knew I was a flake.
I cannot calm my soul
Even for heaven's sake.

She has cried for me,
Eyelashes fused shut.
I never meant to burn,
But it is not a rut.

My mother is snow.
I am fire.
It is not what you like,
But I am no liar.

I swear to you, Mother,
I hear all you say.
I am not your copy.
I will be your daughter another way.

Ever Ender

Ender realized he never understood the world he lived in as they watched planes carve scars into the sky. How industrial, how unnatural civilization had become, still nipping bits of flesh off of the carcasses of flora and fauna after all of these years. A vulture commanding all of the sky.

Ender thought everything between air and ground should be shared. All that was left was water, which would graciously give but never surrender. Ender tried to tell those around him, but the others would not listen. They did not care if the water became gray or the air became cloudy. From where they stood, they didn't have to look at it. The others smiled at Ender amiably, but he knew he just did not belong with them. So with a quiet goodbye, he left. Ender trekked up purple mountains and climbed up ridged, red rocks. He got lost inside of a volcano and planted new trees with new friends in infant forests. But he did not find his love until he got to the end of the world.

Ender expected the end of the world to be quiet, but it was actually quite noisy, buzzing with life from birds, insects, fish, and plants. He didn't expect anyone to announce his arrival, but nothing seemed to notice him there. Unlike most men, this made Ender smile. He had been searching for this place all of his life.

As he sat there, hour after hour, basking in a universe that felt like it was made for him, he started to become lonely. Not necessarily for anyone he had met before, but for a presence he knew was out there and had longed for, reaching his soul out to her as far as it would stretch. He wondered what its touch would feel like as they finally connected. Would he moan at her warmth or jerk away from her cold?

"Hello," a small, subtle voice cooed to him, causing him to jump unexpectedly. A woman carved from the sea stifled a laugh before him. This made a smile tug on the corners of his lips.

"Who are you?" he asked, admittedly a blunt—even rather rude—first question. But she was still smiling.

"I am Ever. The waves lapping beneath her brought her closer to him. "What are you?" she asked curiously. She was so sweet yet just as rude as him.

"Flesh and bone," he answered, standing up to meet her eyes, taking in her glorious, translucent form. He wondered if his hand brushed against hers if she would feel it the same way as he did. "You are not." He was not trying to point this out, but also was not asking.

"I do not believe I am." She was deeply amused by him. "You and I are made up of entirely different things."

As if Ever had been wondering the very same thing Ender had, the two of them brought their hands up as if they were going to shake with their palms facing the others. When they brought them together, Ever and Ender felt entirely different surfaces.

Ender's lips parted as his skin met Ever's for the first time. The cool, cloudless water gave his spirit a pause. He felt as if he would be stopped in his tracks forever. She refreshed him. His posture straightened and his eyes focused. They searched her face for every thought she ever had. He wanted to drown in her embrace.

Ever had to hold herself against jumping back in surprise at the exhilarating heat of Ender's hand. His heat filled her with steam. This change of form so suddenly terrified her. She closed her eyes and imagined herself running away at top speed, her lungs puffing against the cold air and her feet pounding away at a hard, unforgiving ground. Something she could never do. Her limbs surged with force.

They each folded their thumbs over the other's hand, sealing a silent promise of fate between the two of them. Ever and Ender's eyes were smoldering as they memorized the landscapes without defect that made the other's absolute face.

Ever pledged herself to the upkeep of Ender's paradisiacal heart and her sea began to overcome him, pressing them together. Ender lent himself to a lovely paralysis, forgetting he was not born to breath underwater.

Inkling

I don't know what to say when you ask me where I go
When my less than starry eyes glaze over in the distance.
I would not know how to describe it to you.
I don't know if you have ever been there.

I have only ever gone and come back alone.

I think I was still young when age and cracks began to spiderweb my
    porcelain mind.

Thin and fine, my porcelain is an heirloom, passed down for
    generations.

But from my father, I have inherited a skeleton of industrial steel
And so I am an odd creature indeed,
Not overly pleasant to lay with.

My mind is crackling and my bones are creaking as my heart pumps
    hot, black ink for my veins and off to my fingertips.

Sometimes, they envy me because I am made from something
    different,
But loneliness is not a game.
Every time we embrace, it takes something more from me.

I may be cold to the touch,
But most of me will never break.

Brothers Mine

Good, sweet things that somewhat resemble me.
Such honest boys we hope to please.

I know, boys, you think my jokes are less than funny
And that you roll your eyes behind my back as I act like your mother.
But know this:

I remember the days when each of you were born.
Even at that small age as I held your fragile, pink hands.
I saw lifetimes of adventure.

I still remember playing peekaboo with the middle in his crib,
And the younger's chubby toddler legs dancing with glee on Mom
    and Dad's bed.
Even as you grow to be men, those are the things I see.

I do not want to cradle you,
I only want to believe you will be safe and happy always.
That you will remain brave and loving, facing a vast world with wide,
    starry eyes.
That you will find love and conquer continents
Or stay warm every winter night in happy homes.
Do not even let me write your stories.

But as you grow to the men you were born to me,
I will be beside you as long as you want me.

Alma

Alma, dear,
I can hear your music from here,
Bouncing off of the supple clouds,
Raining down on us and sliding off of the leaves.

What do you think of us down here?
One hundred years ago you were my age
And I am grateful for how lives have changed,
But many of us still know your fears.

Do you know me from where you are?
Have you joined the stars?

Language of Fire

Lapping by your toes
With messages to your nose.

Leaving you deliciously free.
How you were born to be.

You are who they fear
When curses come near.

An all-consuming spark
Igniting in the dark.

Get used to the havoc I wreak
And sensuous moans when I speak.

Lady of the Lake

It's funny, isn't it?
How little stupid memories stick to your skull like pancake batter
No matter how many times you try to scrub it clean from the last
    person who stained you.

She mentioned your birthday yesterday.
We have banished you away to some clandestine mortal hell,
Yet here you still remain.
As if we were never meant to win.

You have spoiled all of my memories of you
And yet they still come to me from time to time.

Can you ever really hate someone who meant the world to you once?
It's hardly fair.
Your egoism continues to win because my witless heart cannot bear
    to leave anything behind.

I doubt you know the value of what you did
Or if anyone reading this will see the portrait behind the words.
Friends cut deeper than boyfriends.
Your heart is not prepared ever to lose a friend.

Boyfriends can be like change at the bottom of your purse:
A good one will stick with you for a while
But if you lose track, you will not remember where they were spent.
Friends are like a favorite pair of jeans.
When you wear them, you smile more.
They may as well be a cape,
Giving you familial confidence and care.

You eviscerated my favorite pair of jeans
And yet,
I remember your birthday, too.

Last Things

Can you hear me from here?
I am calling to you from across a flaccid ocean.
I am burning inside out from a fever in my bed.

Do you know what you do?
Sweet and precious you?

My hunger is lasting and my white palms are bare.
I should be running for help, but I am hypnotized by the scar on
    your hand.

Your phantom breath on my neck gives me chills
And it is making it hard to focus.
I will carry that chill along with me to too much time.

It is so important for me to cross that ocean
To take to the end with me the last things I know.

Orchestra

You sigh and I wince.
You swore to me and I swore at you.

You will need to speak up if you want me to hear you.
I am still living with you from two years ago.

I am not ready to face the orchestra of chaos that proceeds us.
Did no one tell us being in love as an adult would be a happy occasion?

My Blood

I am bursting out with feelings and senses,
Wrapping them up like a newborn.
Every time you see me, I am exploding one way or the other.
I cannot waste a thing.
My greatest fear is nothing.

Victory

Blood is pouring from me as it usually does
And it is all I can smell in the air.
Each day, my mind is hazier and the wind is louder.
I have waited one hundred years,
But the wait was worth it.
I was born for this.
Darling girl, do not be afraid.

Honora

Why can't I be bad, baby?
Selfish and covered with filth?
I want to thrash and be unreasonable.
To disappear without a word.
To screw the consequences.
I cannot believe in my heart that I was made to please princes.

Vulgarian

I am pulling as hard as I can to bring my light through these dark
woods you have brought me to.
My feet are moving so fast they are barely touching the ground as I
force myself through.
The bark on the trees is scarred by your reaching arms.

Single-Hearted

"We are only a moment."

You are so kind to remind me, darling. Otherwise, I may have forgot.

I am drowsy because of you.

I made the decision to leave your bedroom before you woke up, but I left my mind laying on your pillow. If you could see it, it would be my goodbye note.

I am a zombie through my day, running my fingertips along the lines around your eyes and grazing the creases in your forehead with my lips.

They hold on to each other, shaping the landscape of my mind that is constantly playing behind my eyes.

I wonder if it was hard for you to get up that morning. If you sat in bed longer than usual, your eyes lingering where I was. I wonder if it was hard for you to let last night's moments go, knowing they were gone because of me and not you.

Roland

What a sweet, lovable child I am,
Or so they all say.
Only I am not a child anymore.

When I tell them I want to be something,
I may as well say "space princess."
"What a sweet girl."

I plead with my father.
I know what I am sacrificing to be creative.
This lovable cherub.

I can already read the life waiting for me
And I trace it in essays to my professors.
"What a bright child!"

Even you, Roland.
If I looked you in your lined eyes and told you,
"You are a pile of diamonds!"
"Aren't you precious?"

Terraform

I am standing under a silver sky.
A desert flower growing against the sun.
My lips are dry and cracked,
Burning against the salt flats.
White seas swell around me.
A pregnant pause is held hostage on my lips.

Finally, I am here.
An alien being.
I do not belong anywhere else on earth.
As the sun descends, the horizon is lavender
And a chorus of breezes begin as I make my way across the raw sand.

Amethyst mountains flank me, but I can hardly tell.
The temperature is low
And my linen dress is nothing.
I am in the devil's playpen,
Yet in the dark, I am smiling.

Blellum

Anyone could forgive you for losing yourself in those rich blue eyes.
Delicate and grand,
You were enraptured by her grace,
Poised for a divine adventure.
The first draft of a breeze and she floated away,
And you were surprised.
Pretty soul,
Your loneliness wounds me,
But then your naivete wounded you.

I will not argue with her:
I am a moth.
Most will not find me beautiful,
But I was born to survive.

Iceblink

What is that rancid light shooting through my scattered brain?
How dare you reach me even here.
I want rage and cruelty to wrestle inside me.
Take your soothing accent to another part of the globe.

You are damn right I am sending you away.
This is entirely my place and no place for you.

Hellion

Oh god,
You are beautiful.
And oh god,
You are horrible
And altogether magnificent.
Whenever I am around you, my blood starts pumping.
Finally, I am awake.
When I close my eyes, I can feel it traveling through me
As if I live in a body made of rivers.

You look like a hawk landed with claws longer than your fingers.
There are no whites to your eyes, but that has never scared me.
What scares me are the irrigation canals you are digging into your flesh,
Carrying feeling from one part to another.

Mutilation is meant to be such an ugly word
And yet it is so commonplace most people would simply offer you a
    Band-Aid.
I do not flinch at the word.

You and I share the same eyes because we are made up of the same
    things.
I know grotesque is so much my truth; I scoff when someone calls
    me beautiful.
I can feel in me what has taken up residence inside of your heart.

We are both appalling hawks,
You and me.
But I do not have wings,
So I cannot fly.
Enjoy yourself up there.

Quiver

I reach back into my quiver,
Hoping for a long, steel arrow to deliver your final blow.
But instead, it is filled with wildflowers.
I sigh as I am forced to settle with profanities.

Eyre

Sacred friend,
I knew you held something in you the very first time I saw that I had
  to love.
What you achieve in your life is your business,
But you have already achieved greatness in mine.
You have mystified me.
Frozen me up from the inside out that I cannot explain.
You call out to me daily,
Rising above the common noise.
But I am the only one who hears it.
How maddening.

Beautiful Gems

Never has there been a treasure so precious than moments and time.
What a glorious currency passed between two souls.
If that was all that we sought from one another, we could gift para-
　　dise onto every person we meet.

All I will ever desire from you is the golden gift of time.
To wrap around your stoniness,
Stretching myself as far as I can to shade you like ivy.
We will grow old together but keep each other beautiful.
More and more as the years pass.

Let me in to your paradise.
Share your time with me.
I will sing to you like a lark
And you will praise me like a painter.

Ingrid

You might catch me for a moment twirling by,
Grateful I was lost to a dream.
I have come to this world hopeful,
Happy I was never clean.
I will lay as I grow against the cold iron chairs in the café that are
tough and withered,
Letting the sun kiss my cheek and ready to accept that it makes me
smile.
I hope when we truly meet, I will be dizzy and laughing, barely able
to contain my joy that I have finally found a partner who will
dance, decorated with a silver dragon painted on my back.

The Bird

Silly me,
Following rivers of fire a whole country long.
Scorched earth is my perfume,
And the cries of common families are an unfortunate aria.
This land has never been known to be barren,
And still, I am flying over babies starving.

Sennachie

Is it with elegant white fingers I weave this tapestry?
I do not even know what language you speak.
How do I know I have really skipped a stitch,
Or you just do not see the full picture?
I have cut my fingers so many times,
Let them throb against the cold,
And yet in the last year, I have only gained another row.

Ineluctable

How much thought have you given to the quality of air we breathe?
As you inhale
And it carries your surrounding down
To flutter and land in your lungs.
Where you are is a part of your chemistry.
Makes you up,
Body and soul.
It instructs your mind
And humors your heart.
If you do not like where you are,
You need to go somewhere else.

Liberate

The spirals of darkness come racing for me, their twisted faces in a hellish smile. They always manage to catch me when I am alone. I inhale—their smoky scent raging within me—ready to move on with them trailing behind.

"Clarie! Clarie! Clarie!" they call out.

I raise my arm, revealing the blinding white flesh of my hand and wrist, and they are drawn to it like it is a sun they have never seen. They reach out like they are going to grip me, and yet somehow, they cannot, even when I am not able to fight them.

I wonder if I am truly walking or just limping at this point after being trailing after for so long. I wonder how red the rims around my eyes are and how puffy are my cheeks? If I allow myself to turn toward them, I will immediately be alarmed at their unearthly wide, serpentine eyes. I will never be allowed to look forward again.

Their performances around me are mockingly vaudeville. My life—to them—is a satirical play. I am a wooden doll, ready to be flung about whatever direction they choose.

I try to repeat some of the kindest things said about me that might be true, but it hardly helps since I am walking further from you.

The color of your eyes fills my lungs like air I was meant to be breathing all along. Your lips are against my ear and your hands on me, keeping me steady. Without you, I would have dissolved long ago. I am trapped at the bottom of an ancient well, and you are the moon above, illuminating my escape route.

I let your love build up inside of me, and suddenly, the chemistry of my body is changed. A warmth is escaping my pores, and when I lay my hands on the glowing skin of my chest, my lips grow into my inaugural smile.

I raise my white-hot hands, searing light racing out as fast as it can. Your beloved light I borrowed from you, chasing that evil back into the dark. Forcing those monsters to curl up into themselves, hissing as they scurry away.

You are smiling with me as your love finally sets me free.

Loneliness

A whistle from the wind so sharp, you wince.
A feverish, grimy gray filter over your days.
A stale air that makes your nose shrink.

Lover's Eyes

Luxurious, tumbled orbs of jade,
Swelling with golden splinters.
Hot chocolate swimming down my throat and warming my soul.
A summer breeze that could carry me away with it.
A cloud you cannot take your eyes off of in the sky.

A million blooming years ahead.
A new silk scarf wrapped around my neck.
Two exotic fish circling each other in a bowl.
Whipped cream abandoned on my lips.
A star-shaped scorch mark left behind on my heart.

Affectionate rest found in my bed.
French lilac perfume applied to my neck.
A fragile matchbook hidden away.
A heart-shaped candy box stuffed with letters.
Poetry of my life.

Dreamer's Curse

Facing phantom adventures one after another a whole realm away
As thousands of limp days chase each other through the seasons.

Years have passed, yet my place in line has stayed the same.
Without books, my spirit would be impotent.
Without this pen, I am just a blind wanderer sleeping in a distraught
    train car.
I do not know what my face would lead you to believe,
But I am a filthy vagrant at heart,
And I do not expect to ever belong.

From the Earth to the Moon

I swear with every cell of myself that each particle of this galaxy was sewn together to be seen by your eyes.

If my tongue must be my currency, I will gather every lucky penny across the globe to get my ticket to you.

I truly believe every scream of my heart soars through the atmosphere of this planet to ping against the stars and find its way back down to you.

Astronauts can feel us in that airless landscape.

You will know me when you see me.
A flare in a dress.
When I take your hand, you will catch fire, too.

We always were meant for the sky,
And the sky was meant for us.

Love

Absolutely, positively essential.
Only meant for the wicked and strong.

Penumbra

They would take and take pieces from me—
Sometimes ripping chunks with their teeth—
And then wonder why I did not perform like a whole girl would.

Parcels of flesh do not just grow back again.
Maybe that is why in my spare time, I sink ships.

Minion

There is a wicked thing stalking my land.
Horned and grotesque, he lights fires to call his minions forth,
Rapping their gnarled fingers against my bedroom window,
Hoping to pull me back to shriek macabre hymns as I scar my own
    skin.

My eyes are burned and blinded by his smoke that fills me.
I think I am calling for help, but maybe there is no sound.
My entire home is ablaze—
Fire reaching to lick the moon's cheek—
But there is not a soul with a hose or bucket.
I think my story ends with my body scorched alive.

What is this thing and why does he want me so?
What shall I do to convince him to let me go?

Bewhiskered

Why do I feel like an ancient thing?
Like I remember a time where dreams did not wrestle with machines?
How can I know you are a man who won't want coins over love?
I think I know you, but maybe that is not enough.
I like black clothes and roll-on perfume,
And you twiddle your life away inside of a camera bulb.
My every utterance is hoarse and yours are Broadway ballads.
You were born to play a prince and I wander the world without shoes.
I am bleeding and limping,
And yet your eyes are still glowing.
Maybe you are not as thoughtful as I took you to be.

Morning Comes

I have swaddled a baby bat with eyes as wide and black as mine,
And tonight, we go to the circus.
I will hold my baby against my chest as we travel against the lights.

It is quite a thing the first time you meet something that deserves all
of your love.

The summer night air is swollen with succulent smells and whirring
lights.
I wonder that they do not realize we have escaped from another cir-
cus quite like theirs.
If they knew that we know, they would never let us see the key more
than once.

Baby, I am yours,
Whatever they think about us sordid beings,
Born to be loved just as they were and less demanding.
Our beauty was described in a language they cannot read,
So they don't realize we are cute for a couple of monsters
Who stand out in a circus.

Tumble Me

My pain is fired back at me,
Dancing on the leaves of all the trees.
My cries are ballerinas with opaline skin—
Leaping as though they aren't from this earth—
Meant to carry on with the stars and born to mock me.
I am a savage being.
Wild—pounding at the ground—
Ugly and severe from birth.
Imagine your surprise when you leave the safety of your home and
    realize that this howl is not coming from a dog.

Univocal

I am leaning over the edge of the boat as you talk to the others,
Wondering who poured paint into the sea.
It couldn't have been born this way.
If everyone knew what this was—
What magnificent possibility laid before land—
They would all be here beside us.

Surprises

You should not have any questions.
I have always made myself open to you, eager to be read.
You ask me things I have written boldly long ago and do not under-
    stand why that makes me wince.
You would have known me if you had just read my work.

Diablerie

Every night when I walk through my old house, my skirt kicks up
    dust.
I wish before they judged me, my neighbors would discover the elec-
    tricity in the air that only the moon can bring.
Then they would see why I slept through the sun.

You are a brave man to sit beside me.
Brave or blessed with simple lunacy.
I know you are wondering as you make eyes at me why I wear the
    face of a hare.
I promise you that I will never tell.

Ossature

I do not know why I am fascinated by my inky black likeness cling-
    ing to the cool stone wall.
Maybe it is because she feels vaguely like me,
Only with a million more opportunities before her.
I will never leave my home.
But as the bird above hurries past, it almost looks like she is wearing
    a coat,
Ready to go.

Evenfall

Maira was the glittering daughter of the Titan Atlas, who bore the night sky. She was so beautiful that she was chosen over a chest of exquisite jewels offered to a mortal king.

They were married, and she took her job as queen very seriously. Maira did anything in her power to fight off plagues and droughts—even sacrificing a delicate and loyal friend to the other gods as payment. Maira put her duty above her own heart. But she did it for far too long.

Maira found that when you neglect your own heart and leave it to starve, it will end up driving you mad. So naturally, she turned to the man she married. They did not marry for love, and did not love each other, still. Only respected each other as man and wife. There was little chance for fulfillment.

For guidance, she turned to her home in the night sky. To her surprise, she saw a rugged, wiry dog. Maybe once, this dog was beautiful, but he fought wars with Odysseus and was scarred and worn. His name was Sirius, and he scared away all who came near him with his angry growl. Maira never saw anything so ugly and was intrigued by this dog. She approached this fearsome beast, and of course, he growled. She still placed her hand on his head, somehow trusting he would not bite. Sirius was stunned, as only the hardened general was unafraid of him. Maira seemed like a beautiful and privileged young woman. Why was she not afraid?

Sirius told her of the other gods who mocked him for his face and threw stones at him, hoping to further wound and take away a whimper with them. Maira began to appear as they did, putting herself in the path of the stones. Never wanting to risk angering a Titan, they would leave quickly and scurry toward other amusements. This action was more than kindness. None of Atlas' other children would protect the hideous dog from danger, no matter the pay offered by sympathizing Odysseus.

Atlas smiled at his tender daughter, feeling the thrum of her heart from the heavens. He changed Sirius into a man, and though he would be just as ugly, Atlas kept his canine eyes and scars so that Maira could recognize him.

Sirius turned the canine eyes immediately from her. Maira smiled.

When they kissed, some of Maira's bright beauty was given to Sirius, transforming him into the brightest star of his constellation.

Maira watched over her husband and children from the sky but never revealed to them where she had gone. For if she ever returned to earth, Sirius would lose his luster and be shot down to the ground by her wounded husband's mortal cannons.

Maira gave up being a great queen on earth for nothing more than the love of a ragged dog.

Cryonaut

Your name never appears without a lyric to praise your beauty,
But that is because they don't see the crooked man sheltered by a top hat.
You are stunning in a sense, it's true.
What I see is a society of twisted bones and a smile of broken teeth.
I can see your phantom kin behind you.
I have noticed that specter holding your hand,
Basking in her nimbus crown.
I don't need you to let her go.
Just allow me to take your other hand so that I can pull you both
    forward.

Glittering Land

What I wouldn't give for a home made entirely of stained glass.
Where I born with a crown, I would have used glass for an entire
  kingdom.

Gorgeous reds and haunting blues,
I would rip off my clothes and bathe in every hue.
A home made of dreams,
Crafted only for me.

Travel Quickly, Travel Well

For a girl so young, I do hardly feel fear.
Perhaps because I have lived a quiet life here.
Born with a suitcase, I know I was meant to go.
To leave behind the world I know.
I eagerly welcome winds of change,
People and places seemingly strange.
Howls and cracks within the walls,
Offensive scribble in all of the stalls.
I smile at each and every one,
And will until the journey is done.
I will treat well all of my hosts,
As I did in the country of ghosts.

Artist

I have had this day marked in my calendar.
Today is the day I eat all of the art in the world to see if I will bleed
clay and paint.

Motel Heart

I do not want to recognize the sky I am under.
I will rid my lungs of dirty air,
Swallowed up by strangers.
My spirit is bare trees and desert.
The exterior is a shocking pink.
This place has color TV,
And draws you in with a glittering neon star.
I do not want to be distracted by life.
I just want to exist.

Naima

The hair on my arm is reaching for the sky.
Why did I think I could survive in this cave?
Waves of stone hang over me,
Intimidating me
And blocking me from any honest light.
I strike this match between us in hopes I can survive.
My flesh is tingling,
Pulling me toward the flame.
This light is not enough to make out the colors of your eyes,
And that is a damn shame.
Is my pale skin radiating against the light?
Are your eyes clinging to my own or my lips?
I hope to become the sun you cannot reach.

Map of Me

Black ink hair bleeding against sand dollar skin.
Onyx sickles hanging above my eyes.
Dangerous, dark orbs they are.
My lover's chocolate twilight.
A slope too deep divides two streams,
Leading to a velvet pillow for your treasured lips to rest on.
A note ended on my hard, marble chin.

Moonstruck

If I have my whole life ahead of me,
Then why am I still bathing in stars?
I cannot see past the fog,
But how is that okay?

All I know is that I have learned to find comfort in my nakedness.

Rococo

I have always wanted someone who also got distracted by the stars,
But maybe we would both float far away together,
Never again seen by our loved ones.
Do I belong on a bed of pink roses,
Or would my heart abuse the luxury?
Your love is ornate
And I am desert sand.

Gadabout

We have just met
And already I am hoping I have overwhelmed your senses.
Grasped you with my shining red lips and lured you in with the
      honey dripping from my fingertips.
Spirals built upon spirals are my eyes,
Hypnotizing you like a desolate snake.
You hope when you see my shoes—
The same dangerous red as my lipstick—
That you know a snare to capture me.
That we will travel together on plush-white sheets.
But are you certain my mind's gaze is on you?

Supreme

Turn away from me you ugly, feral thing,
Glowering at me from that rotting corpse of a tree.
Shoulders hunched, underbite precise: that thing was born for a fight.
Everywhere I go, I can feel her acidic eyes on me,
Burning through my paper skin.
She is judging me:
My posture, my crooked smile, the blackheads on my nose.
Her feline stare knows my every fault and repeats them back to me,
Ensuring—even above the sounds of your voices,
I can still hear them echoing off of each wall before I am slapped.

I Love You

Right as I saw you, it started to burn.
I can't sit still anymore.
It's hard for me to meet your eyes.

I can't open my mouth.
If I part my lips, you will see smoke pouring out.
I can't wag my scalded tongue.

The sharp, sizzling pain is making my eyes water.
I'm clenching my fists, looking around with hopeful and damp eyes.
Someone will put out the chaos inside.
I will swallow aloe and the pain will go away.

The words will scar my tongue,
But at least with time, the pain will fade.

Always Happy

How sweet!
You think I was born to wear expensive jewelry with a smile.

The most important part of my routine in the morning is to glare at
      my reflection and say,
"Suck it up, Buttercup.
The crows are coming."

Prize

The eyebrow scar or dimples could have been what won me,
But with you, it was the mercilessly tumbled hands.
The jagged callouses along curved fingers forced tougher with each
   fight.

I will not hold on to someone who is not rough enough to admit that
   life can be hell,
But that does not mean we will ever understand one another's war.

Armistice

I could not think I was raised to hold decapitated daisy heads in my
      trembling hands.
You must feel the same, too.
Our hands are sticky.
Our backs are hunched, aching.
You would think we loved the dark haloes around our eyes because
      we work so hard for them.

Let's take a breath, you and me,
And send the daisies out to sea.

Bestseller

I hope you miss me with every grain.
I hope flowers are popping up from the drain.

Human Being

I try living with my own kind from time to time,
But it can get a little rabid.
Mostly, I just hide away,
Napping with the wolves.

Wisteria

Your biggest mistake was assuming I needed a palace made of
    diamonds.
That assumption tore us apart,
And all the while, we both knew it.
Maybe I should have just told you that flowers make me happy.

Baby

I am still waiting by the window,
Wincing against the current of the sunshine.
My mind is doing the traveling for me,
Racing above reality and distance.
I never knew until now that the one thing I have been waiting for all
      along was for someone I love to say,
"You have no reason to be afraid.
You have done enough."

Velutinous

Imagine for a moment our return back to nature.
Naked as cherubs racing the wind,
Fingers pink and raw clawing at the ground.
Resting in the wood where you lay,
Worshiping only your own warmth.
Your name is nothing
And everyone you meet is a member of your clan.
Your only need is to make it through while feeding yourself only with
    what you desire.

Versify

I want to hide in a city of a million worlds.
My life should be a blend of too many colors,
Hurting my eyes and even hard to look at.
I will change my name to something like "Zella" and dress like I
joined a hippie movement.
Why limit yourself to only one face?
My favorite piece of jewelry will cost too much and contain a portrait
of my lover's eye.

Strawberry Fields

I was born with the opinion that affection was a scent too sharp and
    distracting.
It would stick to your clothes and become impossible to lose
And then your nose would be wrinkled in every photo.

As I grew into my age,
I have found that love tastes good
And that the intel I have been given was wrong.
It tastes like strawberry lemonade in stifling summer.
I do not even need you to be beside me.
I just hope that your dreams taste as sweet as mine
And that you joyously cling to sleep.

Nadir

I am trying to walk but the tightrope is getting thin.
My intestines are a tangled mess, and I am walking now on floss.
I am trying to make you see that they watch us for different reasons.
I'm not like them, but I can pretend.
My only other option is to walk around looking like a fucking
   catastrophe.

Sunset Highway

I spend more time than I should waiting for a sign of where I will
    end up.
Since I am a writer, you would think I have learned by now that I can
    conjure outward my own life.

Will I end up in an all-white kitchen,
Sitting in a trendy wooden chair cross-legged and sipping lavender
    and cream
While gazing out at my kind of gray day?

Will I be watching the sun set on a road with no sidewalk,
With wind violating my careful hair
As I admire the lights of a city where I never should have belonged?

Miscreation

I do not know if I can love honestly anything that is beautiful.
Especially you.
You have never seen me as I really exist.
My true form is a snarling, panting, growling monstrosity.
I cannot be trusted to take any care.
This human skin is hard to live in.

Truly Trembling

Take me to a place where mountains tremble.
Don't ever say you are afraid of love.
I am supposed to be the coward here.
Let's move somewhere separate from the rest of the world.
No one did seem to like us much anyways.
I like having you near.
I want our shadows to always be reaching for one another.

Viator

Even when I was small, I wanted to believe there was someone out
     there for me to share everything with.
It was not someone to kiss or someone to laugh with,
But I was for them and they were for me.

There are things I have been waiting my whole life to tell you.
Do you think the aches we felt were our skeletons threatening to
     break free from us and run to each other?

I would be satisfied to know that I exist because you were born to be
     shown love.
I am sorry that it took so long,
But I am here for you now.

Heart

I have no one but myself to blame for what I feel for you. I saw nothing but danger in those eyes and yet let my lips smile. I am an intelligent fool.

My Lucah, you are so a part of the sea that saltwater stings in your veins. I still can't believe I was the young girl who fell in love with the gorgeous sailor. If I really am so intelligent, you would think I'd know better than that.

Everything I have ever felt comes down to my first look straight into those otherworldly blue eyes. Where did they come from? Are you even from this earth? They were the natural child of excessive joy and pure ecstasy, and yet I let my lonely self look into them anyways. I let myself linger. But you did, too. Right when they found each other, we should have each let out a volatile scream.

I wonder if you are ever surprised by a desire in yourself to stay with me.

You cup my face in your hands—which reach up to my hair and give me that blasted look of yours before the bullshit comes. "Mason, my girl, I will be home soon." And then I go on with a resentment of the sea. You insist that I am better than that, but I insist that I am not.

Your soul is a wilderness, and I am not done exploring. I have absolutely never met anyone like you before along my entire life. Your zeal and charm are supernatural. You overtook my heart so easily that it forced me to question whether or not I was ever really strong. Is that an achievement you think on when you are alone? How often does your mind go to me when you're away?

What is our destiny that you play for yourself inside of your head? I know there is one. You can't fool me, Lucah. I see it on your face when I catch you looking at me.

I love you, Lucah, much more than anything else.

I don't know if you will see this when you finally bring yourself back. I like to pretend that while you were away, I was not entirely ravenous.

Face Forward

Last night, I had a dream that I was back in high school. Why on earth?

The lone thing I remember from my graduation was barely being able to contain my joy that this journey was finally over. The years of torment were behind me. Those swollen years were not golden, they were layers of heartache. I had many bullies and I will have you know that the physical ones were not girls nor my own size. Finally, at an endlessly long last, I would be released out into the world to find my own people who would accept me for who I am and find something valuable in what I have to offer.

Why are such jagged feelings so hard to let go of?

Why does my subconscious mind want to prove that if I had another go, then things would be very different? I earned my nerve in college when I made friends, whom I still have. Why should it matter that I did not have friends then? I have warmth, laughter, and care in my life now. Why does my body keep traveling back?

How much do those blasted things have to do with who I am?

Mon Cheri

You are lifting a girl high above the ground that was always afraid of
    heights.
I am grasping childishly for the stems of dandelions.
There is dirt under my fingernails
And a flush dawning on my cheeks.
The air smells sweet with fresh-baked bread and old hardcover books.
I am dancing without shoes on the golden sun-bathed grass.
You are wearing a suit and tie, somewhere I have never been.
You are wondering if your laugh is too loud or if your last name is
    right.
That is not my world.
I will meet you in Paris when the first snow falls.

My Great Treasure

They have loved you as a prince but forget so easily that you are a
    man.
Your money is paper,
But your soul…
It leaves me begging for air,
Panting like a mad woman.

You were forged and hammered into being by a Titan of the sky.
Underneath that soft, mortal exterior of man-made beauty, your
    bones are luminous.
My man is as good as gold.

Study of a Young Woman

I dream of being wrapped up in stars,
Looking out at a land I was not born on.
I speak a different language than the people around me
And they watch me eagerly with their heads tilted like a puppy.
My mind is sprinting away from me and my hands are shaking.
Always, always shaking.

Amourshipping

I love to fly,
But what does it mean that I am always crash-landing into your arms?
My hands are reaching high above our heads,
Fingers spread wide:
Little dream catchers that ache for the sky.

You smell like pine
And your grinning brows are ostentatious.
Our chests kiss and then our lips,
And suddenly, we are swimming in paints.
My heart is your playscape.

Land of Stars

There is not a minute of my day without screaming.
All of the colors of my life are swirling together to create something
    I cannot see through.
There is a hurricane in my hands
And my heart is trembling.
You can read both in my private breath.
I am trying to avoid my incoming fate by repeating my own words
    back to myself over and over again:
"You were raised to survive."

Woods Whisper

I am trying so hard to be the lover I want to be, that I am not sure
    what kind of lover I am.
Maybe I am trying to fill in the spaces of my heart that were meant
    to already have been filled by me when we met.
I loved him when I met him.
But then,
I still did love him when I left him.

Metal Bones

One question I cannot stop asking myself even after all of these years is:
Are people even meant to stay together?

My forgiving hand keeps unkind words off of the page,
But who am I saving my soul for?
The people who hurt me most will not read this.

I am shivering always,
Leaving myself bare and in the open,
Yet wondering grimly why I am so cold.

Wolf Woman

When I am home alone, I scream as loud as I can then shiver in the pregnant silence. There are only monsters sitting on my shoulders and they are gnawing openly at my soul. No matter how I claw at my skin, no one ever says if they notice. I teetered at the edge of madness for too many years and now I have finally fallen in. Will you meet me there? You should know before you take the plunge that you will not do it wearing a smile.

There are formidable cuts on my fingers and my nails are too long. You truly think it is in your best interest to hold onto my hand. That is sweet of you, but you haven't felt how cold it is yet.

I have wanted to change my name for years. What could I become? Would it change a thing? What if I ran away to another country with no intention of returning? Would I have to go as me? Would anyone call after me?

You already have a job, golden boy, and it is not to look after me. There is nothing interesting for you to see here, so move along. You already know all I could teach you.

I keep blaming my ugliness on my genes, but maybe it is my heart poisoning my body. I look like the nightmare I see.

Condemned for a reason only I don't know. I was only ever damned by people who could not understand me. Someone should have told them a monster is only a monster as long as you cannot bear to care for it. They hate me, but they created me. Is it my fault they have no self-control?

My hands are shaking, and they hurt terribly from the gashes my claws engraved along the side of my own house. Now maybe the people around me will get the message.

Do you think I am rambling? Does this seem incoherent? Of course, it does! I truly am insane, golden boy, and like it or not, you lay closer to average.

"Cara. Cara, Cara. So sweet. So pretty. Such a good girl. Oh, Cara."

Don't you dare mock me. I will draw back and slash your face. Then you will look just like me.

Someone slashed me once. Ha. One. They told me with an eager grin, "You will scar."

I let myself grin back before I informed them, "I am not afraid of scars, sweetheart. I came from them."

And what difference does that make anyways? Charm yourself how you want, but we both know that one sweet day, not as far away as you would like, I am going to forget your cursed name. It will slip like a breeze right past me without my notice. So take your fill of my nectar and try to forget that you ever saw my boney body naked. If you can.

Do your best to hide the surprise from your face. I know you do not want to be vulnerable. Of course, I am broken, golden boy. What kind of silly question is that? Clearly, you have not been paying attention to the right things. Did you not hear your parents whispering when I was around? I did. I have been long misused. That is what happens after time. Dents gather, people lose their luster, buttons get jammed. I am just an old remote control.

Except I was folded into a wolf. Hide your livestock.

First Builders

Do you think who we are is set from birth?
If we could go back and be abandoned when we were too young to
    remember if we were born somewhere beautiful or terrible,
Would we grow to become the same thing
Or radically different?

Would you still see me the same way under a different sun?

The Moon Metal

Stitch me back together.
Complete me under the harvest moon
On the floor of the woods.
Neither of us mind the beauty of the other.
Chase me through the trees.
Swallow some midnight air.
I hope you can sense how taut the rope between us is
And that you would draw it closer with your hands rather than your face.
I will not come any closer for the cleft in your chin.
The dirt beneath our bare feet is solid.
I need you because I want you.
That is it.

Cotton

The birds and I do not mind each other.
They watch me read and I listen to them sing.
You do not need to know what I look like.
Just imagine a girl who smiles when the bird's gentle singing breaks
    slices through her focus.
Imagine a girl comforted at the sound the breeze makes against her
    trees.
Who struggles to hold her book open at the force of the cars racing
    down her street but still reads in the same spot day after day.
A girl who admires the flowers she pushed through days that burned
    to plant in her garden,
And who smiles in her summer dress against every roasting level of
    sun.

Rapture

Where the hell have you been?
I have been waiting all this time for you.

Let's create a world where Wednesday is the day we sneak away to
    make love under a lavender and peach sunset.

Shelter

I wear nothing but silver armor polished so intensely bright not because I want you to look at me, but rather so that you would not be able to stand it with a grin. I want you to flinch away before you catch a real glimpse. I even carry a sword dotted with opals.

Whenever I am hurt, I make the offender polish it even brighter so that the next person will struggle even further.

I am small inside of the suit and it wears me like I am just the skeleton to an actual body. It is so heavy that I have trouble catching my breath, but I match your smile if you ask after it. Not everyone does anyways.

I was keeping my gaze forward, going on my way when I ran right into you. You did not even stumble, just straightened me up and checked your hair in the reflection of my breastplate. My abiding lips actually hung open. Your face met mine and gave me this cruelly alluring, mischievous grin.

"Alaric," you offered.

"Brynn," I said pointedly back.

It should not have hurt so very much, but it did. To watch all of my painstaking work go to nothing.

Sweet Bones

I should not feel this weary at my age.
I know I am something strange underneath my scarred flesh,
But who else could tell?
When the others glance this way, I cannot bring myself to lie to
     them, even when my heart begs for affection.
"There is no light in here, darling."

I have nothing to give anyone but myself.
They all give me a side eye like they know exactly what that is worth.

Liquid Dragon

I asked you if I was a dragon or roses.
You thought it was so cute I considered that I could be a dragon.
    That my tender heart could be brought to spewing lava and ash.
You called me the rose of your life.
What is that worth?

You doubt still the fire that rages beneath my translucent skin,
Refusing to see anything but my gentle parts.
Neither of us can help that one day, you will be swallowed whole.

You make my heart blush
And that is a dangerous thing.
One day, I will be ravenous:
Sick of my ribs sticking out of my skin and poking me while I try to
    sleep.
And silly you will be sitting there with a wide smile,
Smelling the most delicious of all.

Dislocated

Do not waste your time searching my face.
What you are looking for vacated long ago.
I am not sure if you are brave enough to stick around, but
I will prove to you that even a statue can bleed.

Naked Heart

Nakedness is absolute bravery and daring:
A state I dream nightly of becoming.

What a thing it could be.
For every card I have ever had on display like sobbing art,
So everyone I ever meet will be well-informed
And know their way around my heart.

Mourning Dove

What evidence do I have that I have ever really existed at all?

Despite the times I have made them laugh or the favors I have
    granted,
They act like I have left town with the change of the season.

Forcing a smile never helps.
It wounds too deeply to just be forgotten.

Nightbreath

Ursa kissed my tears away before
Canis wrapped a blanket around my shoulders to stop my shivering.
Orion puts her finger under my chin to lift my head as
Scorpius tells me they don't deserve me anyways.

Cassiopeia grabs my hands and lifts me up.
Lyra dusts off my clothes.
Crux gives me such a stupid grin; I have to smile too.
Lepus leads me away from the spot I cried for too long.

Corvus has a word with my father.
Cepheus looks on soberly.
Draco says I can stay at his place.
Pyxis promises there is more out there than this.

Heterography

He paused as if to say, "I remember you,"
But then he was gone.
So that was worth nothing to me.
Love is not always easy, but it is always love.

I laid there,
Still as I could be—
Begging for God to save me.
I am sick of this.
It should not be raining even though the sun is out.

Spiderwebbed

My nails feel like they are going to break down the middle,
But that will not stop me from grinding them into the dirt.
Blanched skin stretches across a jagged fortress.
I am naked and alone in the woods because I chose to be here.
Your pack does not scare me.
I have already died once.

Your beryl eyes count for nothing in the wild.
Don't you dare corner me.
If you try, I will carry a piece of you away.

I know how long the night lasts.

Ghastly

I know from the weight of this devilish thing on my chest that I will
    never sleep again.
It is a twisted cherub that mocks as it smothers.
I am hanging over the edge of my own bed,
Eyes bulging,
And even midnight beasts look on in horror.
The hem of my skirt twists and locks my feet in place.
My neck aches as my head weighs it down.
My consciousness is displaced.

I will never sleep again.

Tempest

It was hard meeting you.
I could have cried for hours. Maybe I did. I do not remember. Or my
    stubborn and tough heart has pushed that night away.
It was the slaughter of anything selfish.
I will love you severely—
Whatever you do—
Every day for the rest of my life.
The heart truly does ache when it thinks of another before itself,
And mine is throbbing barbarically
As if there is no other world away from this.
Please find your way to me
Before my core devours my forlorn body.

Vigor and Valor

Your baritone chases the serpents away.
Your holy eyes whitewash my instincts,
Forcing them clean.
My boiled heart is wrapped in a satin web.
You are here because you got too close and now you are stuck to it.
You are trying to escape—
To pull yourself free.
But really, it is playing me sweet music like what's left is a violin.

Grief

I do not actually shine.
I am elderly—
Torn clay dipped in glaze.
If you try to drink from me,
All you are looking for will swell at the cracks.

Gasoline for Blood

Pulses race through me from end to end,
Bringing forth questions no one really understands.

I am addicted to the things you have wasted your life loathing:
Namely the way your body refuses to stagnate.
You let them talk for you,
But in between,
Your foot bounces.
Your fingers crack
Once, twice——that's three!
Your water bottle is at your lips.
Must fiddle with your hair.
Give a cautious glance toward the orator, hoping they are not waiting
    on you.
There is the water bottle again.
Now you are looking at your hands.
Are they trembling?
You bite your lower lip as you try to remain still,
But the thick threat of anxiety pricks at the back of your neck.

The water bottle is back.
Your eyes remain carefully still behind the radiant curtain of your hair.
No,
You already cracked your knuckles, remember?
So you trace foreign shapes into your palm.
You are chewing the inside of your lip.

Would it calm you if I placed my hand on yours?
Certainly not.
You would cast a smile on me and your foot would bounce again.
I am deeply entranced and fascinated.
Your middle finger traces your eyebrow.
You straighten the lap of your pants.

Does no one see the chaos?
Are you even breathing?
You are desperate for another knuckle crack.
You run a hand,
Once, twice,
Through your tired hair.
Water bottle again.

Silence.
It is your turn to speak,
And I realize that I am on the edge of my seat.

Barn Woman

It has always been this way in our town filled with porcelain nothings. Like we all were born to see through a foggy lens. There is a lot of aged yellow—like a smoker's teeth—in our decorating and the air wherever you are tastes like stale, dusty crackers. The buildings all around are broken and shaken loose like we were struck with something hard. This is the place I come from.

Naturally, no one would believe it was fairies prowling at night, coming to so gross a place. The people here believe in a monster. A beast so cruel it made a town that maybe once was shiny a deplorable ashtray. That is how people say this happened anyways.

I went out on my own to find this thing. Someone needed to. Why? Don't ask me. What kind of person goes looking for monsters?

It did not take me long. We all knew where it lived: a crooked barn past the edge of town.

I came inside and was surprised by the brilliant light and immediate warmth. The wind beyond kept the barn door knocking against its frame.

The thing barely wasted a moment. It appeared above me in the hayloft, which was filled with soft and golden hay.

It must not have been a thing ever seen before by another living person.

The mortal observation was that it was a large, humanoid barn owl. But I knew it was more. The feathers and wings hung like Athena's commanding robe. It had the hair of a beautiful woman: minky blonde, fading to a warm, earthy brown, flowing like water in ringlets past its chest. Like perfect and welcoming water. Water you have long dreamed of swimming in. The eyes were arrows that shot forth and hollowed out my head. I did not know if they were black, gray, or brown. They were shaped like diamonds men had tried to cut. They failed: the things were deadly sharp. They led to an ancient nose and perfect mouth. The mouth was warm as coals. As the earth's core. It was shaped like a heart—so loving and inviting as all women's hearts surely were. Whatever it was, it could not have been born on this earth.

"What is your name?" it spoke to me.

How many years have I been standing here?

I longed to be brought against its chest by the gentle ease of their elegant and forgiving wings.

"Fionn," I answered. I thought it was smiling.

"Thank you."

"For what?"

"It makes it more convenient to recall my last meal."

I did not believe it. I did not even hear it. I was touching its face with my eyes until it lowered itself to me. It was umbrage.

I closed my eyes, never to know how it decapitated me with its wings and swallowed me whole like a boa.

Lover, Mine

Lover, mine
I cannot, will not go.
You are a novelty to them, and I will not leave you alone.
I was caught as I felt the brush of your soul,
Wandering the earth still looking for a home.
The soul of a man who still sleeps on trains.

When we met, our palms kissed
And your smile reached your eyes.
I sighed.
"Dammit."
You caught me.

We rarely leave your home.
We just enjoy keeping each other nearby.
But I fell watching you at the window.
You were so focused,
Miles from here.
It was then
When I realized you were also the kind of person who watches storms
That I knew I could love you.
You are a man who looks for beauty in chaos.
I am a woman who would cherish that.

Who Is She

You have caught me at a time when I am drinking little more than
    moonlight.
In the middle of my lycanthrope transformation, I am naked, but I
    am still human,
Laying like a child in the leaves, perfectly pathetic.
There is a glint in my eyes folks do not know how to trust.
Do I seem dangerous to you?
Are you afraid?
I only mean
You thought I was a sweet dog,
But I am actually a wolf,
So while you are gone,
I am going to destroy all of the furniture
And maybe eat your pet.

Yearning

I am not for everyone,
But I hope I am what you have been waiting for.
I cannot just bat my eyelashes.
My heart is not in it.
Whoever loves me will have to take on more than dainty hands:
Traumatic highs and lows
Are the gifts of my soul.

You will struggle to know me completely
And to protect me exhaustively.
To hear:
"This is what makes me ugly."
"This is why my hands tremble."
"This is the only way to get my smile to reach my eyes."
"Let me tell you why you are so perfect."
"Be careful with that life of yours that is so precious to me."

Outré

I understand that I was born to carry the weight of my head,
But I never expected as I grew that it would come to weigh so much.
Expand so fully beyond the limits of human need.
Slow to heal from sluggishness,
Bursting at the seams from frivolity.
Why am I so surprised at my anxiety?
My mind was meant to be a wild, carefree thing.

Wilder

I am intoxicated fully after dancing on a trail of stars.
I twirled with such joy that you saw the full length of my white legs
And my skirt spread up and open like flower petals.
My small fingers tangle in the air above me as if it is my lover's hair.
My curls are a hopeless, black blur.
I will dance alone if you make me,
Or you can take hold of my heart with foolhardy moves.

Fortifying

Some might say I am projecting,
But it does not really matter when I feel something so strongly mov-
    ing around in my heart—
Like a creature in a womb too small—
Does it?

How can I tell you that you are the adventure I have been looking for?

Earthshaking

I am claustrophobic and never knew it.
I am torn between being desperate to move and not lifting my legs.
I am suffocating myself.
Why am I so sad?
Is it because I am realizing I actually have feelings?
Why am I eager for a place that does not exist?
I will never have that life because it simply is not real.
Even though I can see this,
Why don't I know it?
Has anything I have ever wanted been real?
We are so focused on "becoming" that we forget about "existing"
    which is—
Despite what anyone will tell you—
What we were born to do.
To exist as we are.

Isolato

Can you imagine yourself contained in woods with a gray sheen over
        everything—
Alone and naked in the water?
Do you think it would be a bad thing?
You are anything yet nothing out there because
The woods do not care if you live or die
And there is no one around to answer to.
I think being alone out there would do things to me.
I would answer to another name and never cut my nails so I would
        leave marks on everything.
I would let myself believe the water was in love with me,
Even though it races through my fingers when I cup my hands.
Inside of it, my back would arch and my legs would float.
I would let myself become this dirty, lazy, feline thing
And no one would recognize me again.

Please excuse me.
I am made of dreams.

Midnight Mystery

I am walking along,
Secured in clothes much too tight
And with a bat pulling at my knotted, wild black hair
As if to say,
"You are not meant to be beautiful,
So quit forcing yourself to want it."

Rare Beasts

I spread my arms out first and then my legs as I drift along the perfectly clear blue-green water. I spread my palms upwards as exposure to the surface tickles my bare breasts.

I float by a man minding his own business and I want him to look at me. To notice I am naked before him and smile because of it. I already have a man to be kissed by, but that does not stop my greedy, mundane heart from wandering. I want to be loved by him because I do not know who he is or what he is made of. Do you ever find someone who answers all of your questions for you? "My name is Koa..." I want to purr. But I do not. Because that would be wrong.

I twist onto my belly and start moving my arms and legs so they will bring me forward. The line of water is at the bridge of my nose and yet still, I open my mouth. To eat, I tell myself. I take in water lilies and though they smell fragrant, they taste bitter. They did not even begin to fill me and only really made me realize the hollowness of my stomach.

Maybe my mistake is thinking I could be content just floating along. I have imagined all this time that I wanted to be like a mermaid, but I have forgotten about what walking on the cool morning grass feels like.

Fitz and the Heartbreaks

There is a lot of pain in being a giver.
You are used up faster
And end up emotionally catatonic.
What's worse:
A giver is usually forged by takers
And therefore, learn to cope with loving them.
Accept the injustices of their life as "normal."
This is an efficient process because they have a choice,
But a giver cannot become a taker because it goes against the purpose
    they have been given in life,
And so they have nothing left because by the time they realize what
    has happened,
The purse of their heart is empty
And their voice is quiet.

From Me to You

Near or apart,
I adore your heart.

From here to there,
My heart full of care.

I take your hand,
For a better land.

From me to you,
My heart always true.

Selene

Moon and stars
Beneath my scars
Shining through
In perfect view.

My secret pain
Drives me insane.
My confidence slain
By echoes in my brain.

Sugar

There is darkness hidden
Where love was forbidden.
Before our sweet start
I guarded my heart.

To heartache I was prey
In that brute place I stay.
I thought it would never end:
My will would have to bend.

I hope it is worth it all—
Every hurt, every flinch.
You are my own espresso shot.
I am your richly sweet spot.

Hello, Again

"I might seem like a stranger, but really, you do not love me yet."

I can still picture his crooked grin the first time he spoke to me. When I close my eyes, I can still see his cobalt-blue eyes challenging mine. Oh, how my blue heart bleeds.

Grayson was the man I could love and the person I could trust. He took turns making me crazy or shining, and I am still not sure which he enjoyed more. He was the Lancelot of my life: chivalrous, daring, bold. More impressive to me, still, was the gleaming empathy. When the occasion came for it, he held a warmth like no other. At the first sign of dismay, we would stroke my cheek, brush the hair from my eyes, and tell me everything is going to be all right. My heart would quiver and forget all of the wrong in the world. But now my heart is frozen.

They called it Black Lake because it seemed bottomless. It was dark that even when the brilliant summer sun shone directly on it, still, you blearily made out your own reflection. It was a jar of spilled ink. It just seemed right to come here. This is where I loved to go with him. It just felt like it belonged to me now, somehow.

Remorse is my new suitor I never hoped to love. But I cannot deny he is the one who holds me close in the night now. It is him that holds my hand when I walk through the halls and hurts my neck as I read. He is always with me, taunting me because he is not Grayson.

"You are my special girl, Aria," it echoes in my ear.

"I love your words. I love reading you."

I am vacant: the world is hazy and I could evaporate at any minute.

I even loved him for the way he left me.

My Grayson was always the one who saved me, so it was not a surprise he would die someone else's hero. He was the only one brave enough to stand between two angry, thoughtless people. My heart swelled so that my chest began to tear and bleed. I knew from its birth it would be different this time. With a few fatal words, he was gone and now my life is little more than a crack in a frozen, winter window.

I am standing at the edge, staring down my own reflection in the remorseless water. No one really gets it. They all say they do, but they do not know what I have lost. "She is just sad," they say. "She needs some rest. She will be better with time."

For days and days, I have sat, trying to remember how it was I went on with life before him. I do not know what I am anymore. I am waltzing for hours with a candle in my hand. My fingers are scorched to the bone and my feet are pathetically bleeding. My partner is cold and dead. I have danced with him for so long and yet he only has eyes for me. He thinks I am beautiful and kisses me every chance he gets.

The water is cold and soothing. I will be reborn. I will be saved. This will not be a "goodbye." I am not sad. My tears can finally stop as I clear my throat to say, "Hello, again."

Sugar Storm

Find me in a sugar storm.
I will keep you safe and warm.

Think of me between heart beats
And look for me in the streets.

Green eyes call to view
Every way we're blown to.

Rosy cheeks and a sugary kiss:
Things I never want to miss.

I will give my heart willingly and true,
And work to win the love of you.

The Dream of Eve

Return to heaven
At your heart's content.
I know I am a part of you
And therefore, never alone.

He cannot convince me
I was not created
To look into those eyes.
They strike me to my soul.
They're the only gospel
I need to know.

Born subservient by
The will of your rib.
At my creation
He did not know
He made a kingdom
Inside of these twisted bones.

Brass Mill

Such a haunted place.
My heart swells.
A smile grows on my face,
Though it's burnt like nine hells.

In my heart, this place is divine.
I watch the light dance on the walls.
I am desperate to call it mine.
When I leave, my heart falls.

I listen to the birds
And the crunch of the glass.
I am always lost for words.
My heart is made of brass.

I want to take you here one day.
We will smile and together we will stay.

Blackbird

I have stayed in this steady, unchanging place I have grown.
Reaching my hand out desperately for a journey of my own.
I despair and ache for the many places my mind has flown.
For the premature funeral of my heart only recently sewn.
I daresay no amount of flight will dissolve me intimidating tone.
My feathers are black so you will spot us: I will not be alone.

Fire Is Free

Flames stretching,
Slapping the sky.
Fire can be free,
So why can't I?

Hunger burns,
I hunt and steal jars.
The bombs burst and echo,
Reflecting from the stars.

The men in gray
Bark every demand.
But there's fire here,
A sign God's in command.

It forces them back.
There's no water to throw.
They have no choice:
They must go.

The city groans
With bursts of light.
My head is high.
I will survive this fight.

Miles and miles,
My journey stretches on.
The war is over.
We are not gone.

I knew he was watching.
I knew God would see.
Now fire is free,
Just like me.

For Abraham Lewent, Holocaust survivor (1924–2002)

Rosaleigh

Her little hand shivered as she placed it on the cold door. The room was completely silent. Her nerves were in tangles as if she was breaking the law. The door opened with an ungodly creak, and the smell enraptured her. It felt like the comfort of a warm fire and old books. Rosaleigh stepped in slowly at first then altogether. She smiled, taking in the comforting red walls and smooth hardwood floors.

Rosaleigh ran to the bookshelf and took out *The Picture of Dorian Grey*. Father had a room filled with books, but he only pretended to read everything else, and Rosaleigh knew that. When she opened the book, the binding squeaked and the thin pages felt as if they would disintegrate under her touch. She placed the book on his desk, opened to the last page he had read. She also took out his pen and clicked it a few times as her father did when he fiddled with it as he read along. She placed it beside the book and took her father's jacket off of the chair. It was an old and well-worn brown leather jacket. It smelled like him and that fact made her smile. She draped it atop her shoulders as he would and held it closed. She went next to the bookcase and took out the prettiest colored book and brought it to the window seat. She pretended to pour over the pages with the same look of concentration and occasional bursts of wonder she had seen her father wear a hundred times. Of course, she could not understand the words. She was only able to enjoy the illustrations.

This was the last place that felt right. The house had been silent and cold for a while now. Mother did not talk much and no one seemed to ask why. Rosaleigh played on her own for hours and then went back inside. She hated the frigid stillness of everything but loved her mother too much to risk disturbing her peace with questions. It had been that way since the morning her mother came in and told Rosaleigh her father had gone away to live with the holy virgin. She did not know why her father left, but she wanted his room to be perfect when he came back. She wanted him to be proud of her trying to read. She could not concentrate on the book however.

Outside the window, lived a wild array of vibrantly colored roses billowing in the breeze. They were starting to become frail with age and lack of care. Outside seemed like a magical land to Rosaleigh. The smell of the roses did not touch this room. Inside here, it smelled like raspberries and wildflowers. On special days, it smelled like a lit fire. When she closed her eyes, she could picture the flames crackling and making the shadows of the room dance.

When she came up with a story based on the pictures in the book she knew her father would like, she got up and walked over to the record player. It was very large and ornate, and normally Rosaleigh would not be allowed to play with it, but she knew somehow her father would make an exception for her this time. "Everywhere you go, Rosaleigh, you shall have music," he would say to her.

She picked up the needle and placed it on to the record that never changed. *"Hold me close and hold me fast, this magic spell you cast…"* the record sang. She expertly recalled the story her father would tell her about how he and her mother danced beside the roses to this song, and that was how Rosaleigh got her name. She pictured her father showing her how they danced and holding her little hands in his as she balanced on his feet. She sighed and smiled. Rosaleigh could not wait for her father to come home. *"Give your heart and soul to me, and life will always be la vie en rose."*

Odette's heart weighed heavy as she pressed her ear to the door. It broke her heart to see her only child in such a state. She did not know what she could say. Who was she to break this trance? Rosaleigh was young and naïve, and this fact protected her from being broken. Odette did not even know how to do it. She would stare at her child's touching hazel eyes and the words would spill out uncontrollably. What would come out?

She placed her hand on the doorknob and immediately froze. Odette felt a shock rocket up her arm as if the door had electrocuted her. She felt as if she was not supposed to be there. She just knew if she were to open the door, her husband's ghost would rush at her, finally finishing her off. Odette knocked lightly on the door and heard the record stop. Rosaleigh shuffled over and cracked the door open. She looked as though she had gotten into some trouble, and this made Odette smile at its familiarity.

"Won't you come with me to lunch? I will make anything you like."

Rosaleigh nodded her head and gingerly shut the door. Odette took her hand and led her across the house.

They both ate in silence. It was as if one knew the other was hiding something but they were, too. When lunch was over, Rosaleigh ran outside to play and Odette remained frozen in her seat. Her body felt cold and she had to remember to breathe. And then, finally, it all became too obvious.

What would Henry do? He had lived his whole life as her muse, and she became all the warmer inside realizing his job was not yet done.

Odette went outside and smiled at her daughter, gesturing for her to come to her. Rosaleigh came to her with her hands behind her back, biting her lip, and looking to the ground.

"I'm sorry I went into his room, Mama."

"Whose room, Rosaleigh?" Odette asked.

"Daddy's," Rosaleigh answered quietly.

"Why don't you want to say his name?

"Because Esther said that whenever anyone says Daddy's name, you cry, and I don't ever want to make you cry, Mama."

Odette's heart swelled and she felt her hands shake.

"Don't you worry about that, my love. I am only sad because I am going to miss Daddy."

"Don't worry, Mama. He will be back soon," Rosaleigh said, sweetly taking her mother's hand.

"You will see him again, Rosaleigh, but not for a long time. You see, when the holy virgin asked Daddy to come to her, she did it because he was the very best writer in the whole world and they wanted him to tell stories to all the little children who live in the shadowlands. They do not have anyone to look after them, and so they asked if they could borrow him."

Odette waited nervously as Rosaleigh furrowed her brow.

"That's nice of Daddy! They can borrow him, Mama. I think that's good of him. I just want to keep you."

Odette squeezed her little girl's hand with a sob.

"I am not going anywhere, baby."

Lady Greensleeves

Why are we not together in the grass right now?
You are my breathing lucky charm, and I am your bright girl,
After all.
What do we imagine we will gain with success?
Life is short and I have been happy poor.
We belong to a unique time of personal freedom and open joy.
We could take our savings and not come back until all of our clothes
have grass stains and there is a constellation of freckles across
our cheeks.
If we do not waste our days kissing in the sunshine,
I have failed you as a lover.

Wormwood

I am one of the lucky ones.
I am half alive.

I am sitting,
Digging my feet in the sand,
Waiting for the tides of change to greet me
Finally,
Like an old friend.

I would like to think I carry a heart of dignity,
Happy with gold or tinfoil.
I have settled fair with both.

If I lay carefully on our bed, will you tattoo me with watercolor paint?
I am optimistic.
My mind dreams midday through rays of a summer sun.

To Sweet, Holy Ezra

I know full well I am wasting my time.
But still,
I hope you got my paper plane.
There are words inside
I wrote specifically for you.
They basically say:

Your smile makes me smile.
You seem like the kind of guy who gives a crooked smile with his
     hands in his pockets.
I bet you would wrap around me like a cashmere sweater:
Soft but dazzling.
You invoke driftwood and dancing on tables.
When you put your hand on my cheek, it will feel like a summer
     breeze.
I hope you would like how I would look in your clothes because I
     will stealthily steal them all.
They will come back to you smelling like Daisy Love.

I want to leave you breathless, Ezra,
And full of love.

Simple Wishes

When you asked,
"Who are you?"
I cracked like a mirror.

In your doorway,
I was breathless.
All night, this look
Will live on my face.

I know I will see you again
Because I always come back.
You will know me by then.
If not, I am a failure.

We are a crying shame,
Aren't we?
Two good people should love each other happily.
But this is not a '90s movie.

I will not wake to you with a perfect soundtrack playing in the dark.
Please forgive my foolish heart.

Plexus

How do I share my feelings for you without coming across as com-
    pletely heartless?
You did not ask for this.
You are a fever in my blood,
And I am not sure how much longer I can take it
Before they wheel me away
Muttering to myself.
I just pray he will never catch it.
I will wake up in that room and close my eyes again,
Pleading with myself to remember if it was your name I muttered
Or his.

Maiden Freedom

There is this feeling of mundane peace that I cannot explain to you.
It feels like a freshly painted white wall in a sunny hotel room far
    away from here.
I can see it in my heart.
I am laying my hand on the wall,
Smiling
Because I am somewhere else
Finally.

I Remember Mama

I remember Mama.
I remember Mama before she was your Mama.
I remember clothes pins in jars on the porch
And fireflies sifting through summer dusks.
I remember walking a wooden dalmatian through the gravel drive-
     way against a rented old house.
Even then I treasured peace.

Gypsy Water

I believe in powerful summer nights,
And only coming indoors when you can carry the smell of a bonfire
to your bed.

I believe in that flash of fear and excitement when you embark on
your first adventure,
Desperately hoping for love, friendship, thrills, and color.

I believe in making myself a caravan instead of a house, so I never
have to wake up where I do not want to be.

I believe in love and joy and hope,
And it is important to me that I let people know that those things
are still out there.

I believe deeply and truly in love
And what it could do for us if we give it a chance.

Soft Gloom

One day, you will come to appreciate the color in your life.
I know you did your best,
But the worst thing you can tell a young girl is that what she feels is
      not real.
Your biggest mistake will be thinking that I cannot outrun you.
I can dream of escaping things that I still love,
And often I do.
I cannot bark anymore and
Only dim dogs bite twice.

Bats and Dragonflies

Come to me in the night and let me prove myself to you.
I want you just as breathless as I have been.
All I can see in the world right now is black lace, red lipstick, and
stinging purple neon light bleeding through borrowed curtains.
Are you prepared to kiss me for all of the years I have not been kissed?
Being hopeless is not so bad.
I am walking on air.
I feel more beauty, delight, and chaos than I ever have before in my
life.
I want you to kiss me so that I walk the earth on wobbly legs.
I want to wear bruises on my wrists and knees.
The only honest desire I have is to be swallowed up by love.

Idiot

Someone out there right now could be dying of love for you
And you would never know
Because they would never tell you.

It's me.
I am the one holding my destiny in my own shaking hands,
Yet doing nothing with it.

Can't you see me?
I am burning with love for you.
I am screaming—
Tearing at my hair.
I need you,
And you look straight past me,
Burying a knife hilt deep in my throat.

Idiot,
Look at me!
You're the man I love!
Have you not noticed me calling out for you?
Haven't you heard my crying?
It was coming from the next room.

Gather some courage and find me.
I would never turn you away.
I promise it will be okay.
Just be brave.

Please,
My love,
I am bleeding.
My tears brutally sting, and my head is aching.
I need you.
I want you.

I am praying deeply for you like an idiot
Who does not own a phone.

Strawberry Wine

I will love you always
As much as you deserve.
I hope after we are long gone, people will still trace our story written
    in the whirls of the wood that built our home with their hopeful
    fingertips.
Your warmth was a balm that spread across my life.
I have loved you long and so I know it is love because still
I love you well.

And you love me well.
Your patience and strength are a gift,
Your friendship inexhaustible,
And your affection soft.
I pledged to smile into your eyes every morning of my life,
And I would do it again.
I cry to remember the sight of your miracle hands helping me to
    build the bones of our children.
Together,
Once,
We fell from the dust of the galaxy.
I was beside you before we were born.

I have found the compass guiding my life inside of you.
The wave of you was dizzying from the first moment.
Every muscle of mine was made tender.
How can it be celestial justice that I ever deserved you?
How could I believe such a thing?

If we belonged to another time and another place
And my body still had this soul trapped inside,
I would spend every moment of that life searching for you
And build this exactly as it was all over again.

Hunger

From a young age, I have searched for things golden.

As a child, I would put my tiny hands into the hands of adults.

As a teenager, I would dress like rock stars.

Always looking for something golden.

As a young woman, I imagined romantic love must be golden.

I would sacrifice much too much time on my hair and face because that is how you win people over, isn't it? I would carefully choose my clothes. Four hours gone and now I am ready for someone I do not even know yet.

One morning, I woke to beautiful hands caressing my bare back. I smiled against my pillow and opened my eyes. The morning sun was reaching me from the window. I raised to my elbows and just watched as she rose, burning and giving at her own pleasure.

I got up from my bed and went outside. The grass was cold and my feet were stung by little bugs. I made my way to a hill that stood tall enough to make me a little dizzy.

The first time I reached for her, my arms were still tired and I did not reach over my head. Her blazing skin scorched my fingertips. I jerk my hands back toward me, but I was not deterred.

The second time I reached for her, I was standing on my toes and my palms were open and above my head like a small child's. Her powerful body was in my grasp and my own body began to sway like it was caught in the rough wind. I had to toss her back before I dropped her.

I had to do something before I lost the will to change.

The third time I reached for her, I took on the burning and stinging against my skin with a brave face as if nothing had changed. I hoped to trick my body. I opened my mouth until its joints sang and swallowed the sun whole.

My skin glowed before it snapped.

My eyes shone before they bled.

My heart was warm before it burst.

My name was not Sarah, it was Serena.

I found everything I was looking for before I combusted like a firework.

Lighthouse

My mouth is poisoned by salt.
Sea water is biting my eyes.
I can only grasp onto unforgiving shards of stone.
You are not so far away,
Yet you have not come to save me.
I think I will drown here tonight.

Cobra Kiss

I know we will not last,
But I love you still.
I want my lips to bruise yours so that every time you speak, I am
    with you.
I am dying with love for the last time.
This is what I have lost.

Lady of One Thousand Scars

I am in pain because I am lonely.
Because I place my value on the people around me.

I am lost because I have tried too long to hide in a group.
To pretend their dreams are mine.

I cry because you are the only real love I have ever had
Over and over because of how you have hurt me.

I am anxious because I have never known who I really am.
My life still has not begun.

I bleed because I am human,
Even though I let myself forget.

I will survive because I am strong.
I will not give myself any other choice.

Wellspring

Let me be your mistress.
Let me be your maid.
I will give you sunshine
Cooled by lemonade.
My hope is high:
I have long yearned for you.
My sweetness is an asset
Or so they assure me.
Is that what you saw
Ten years ago?
When someone notices me
I cannot let it go.
Your face has haunted me.
I hoped my petals would wither
Beneath the frost of shame,
But years have passed, and I am still soft,
So here we are again.
I am begging you:
Bring me close or let me go.
I am decaying in between.
I live in a void not of this world
And everyone I love is a dream.

Suitcase

My favorite worn golden yellow sweater
That used to be his sweater.
I only pack the best things when I run away.
Only the things that will make my heart feel like sunshine.
My favorite book—soft from a thousand reads—hidden inside of
  our sweater.
A delicate floral perfume bottle wrapped in a satin scarf I will never
  wear but be happy to have.
Polaroids of us with me much too pale to flip through at night.
Leggings my mom bought me that are not as tight as the ones I buy.
Postcards to make my best friend smile from a world away.
A necklace of Saint Katherine of Alexandria to play with when my
  thoughts dance away.
Wherever I go, I need to bring summer with me.

Handsome Man

Out of respect and affection for you,
I will stay true.
I did not plan for a storm to ensue.
To fall for eyes so deeply, perfectly blue.

Roots twisted around my bones like an ancient tree,
My insides turning like I swallowed an angry bee.
The future is clouded so I cannot hardly see.
These walls did nothing to protect me.

Oh, how his heart surely gleams
Is taking an axe to all of my seams.
It burns me worse than ambitious sun beams.
I really wish he could not read all of my dreams.

About the Author

Sasha Madsen wrote *Lycanthrope* with the belief that if she opens up her own inner workings to her readers, they will feel more comfortable to do so as well. Sasha is a big fan of conversation as well as postcards, ballet, history, sunny yet breezy days, and martial arts. In a perfect world, Sasha would sing jazz and dance excitedly with grinning partners for a living. She hopes by the time this book has released that she will finally have found the perfect place for her black cat clock that beams at her with a wagging tail in her peach-colored bedroom.